A Gift For:

_____

From:

_____

Copyright © 2010 Hallmark Licensing, Inc.

Published by Hallmark Books,
a division of Hallmark Cards, Inc.,
Kansas City, MO 64141
Visit us on the Web at www.Hallmark.com.

Editor: Megan Langford
Art Director: Kevin Swanson
Production Artist: Dan Horton

ISBN: 978-1-59530-305-9

BOK1158

Printed and bound in China
JAN11

Hallmark
GIFT BOOKS

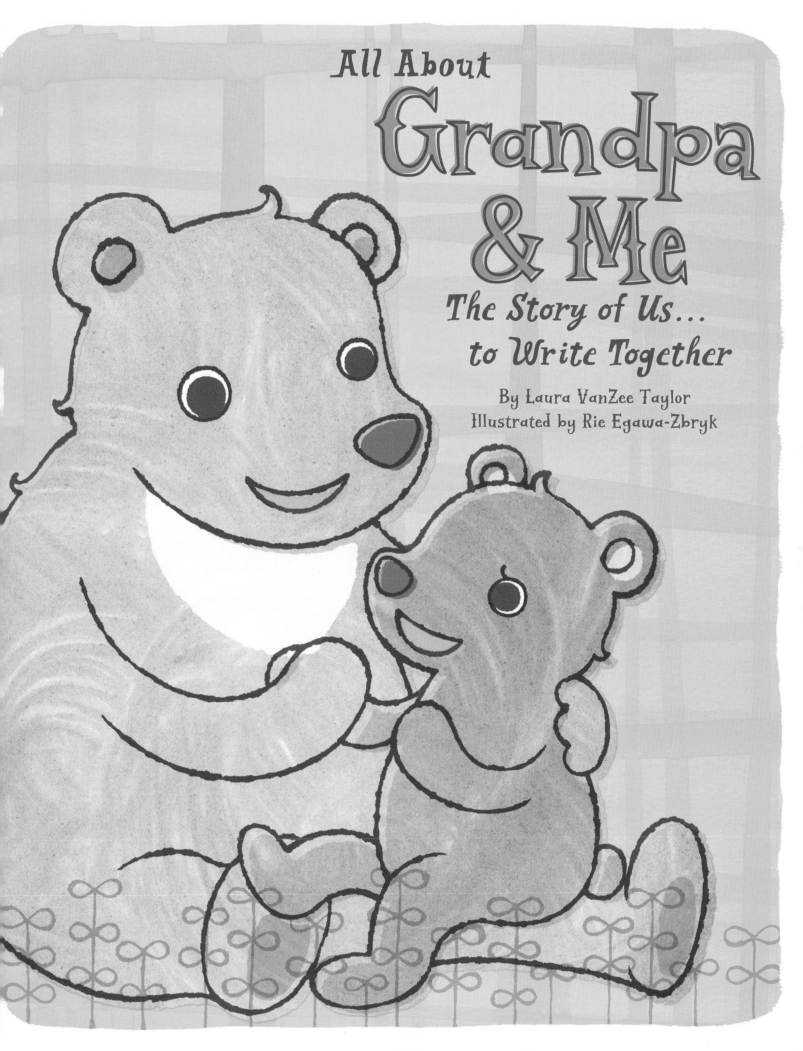

All About

Grandpa & Me

The Story of Us...
to Write Together

By Laura VanZee Taylor

Illustrated by Rie Egawa-Zbryk

To You & Your Grandpa,

Grandpa, Grandfather, Gramps, Pops...Whatever you call him he's an important part of your life. And this book is all about the two of you. It's a fill-in-the-blanks, draw-and-doodle, write-all-over book to complete together. It will help you share tons of fun stuff about you and help you learn a whole lot more about your grandpa. The two of you have a story to tell, whether you know it or not.

Filling out this book makes a great project for a rainy day or a quiet afternoon—whenever you have some time together. Complete it from start to finish or a little bit at a time. Whatever you like! You'll be sure to find something that makes you smile—and you'll end up with an all-about-Grandpa-and-me book to keep forever!

And no matter what, don't forget to have fun!

Full name: _____

Nicknames Grandpa calls me: _____

I was born on _____
                (month)   (day)   (year)

That makes me_____years old.

_____was the president when I was born.

My hair is_____

My eyes are _____

I am_____ tall and weigh _____

My best feature is _____

The Basics

Grandpa's full name: _____

Nicknames I call Grandpa:_____

Grandpa was born on _____
(month)   (day)   (year)

That makes him _____ years old.

_____was the president when Grandpa was born.

Grandpa's hair is_____

Grandpa's eyes are _____

He is _____ tall and weighs _____

His best feature is _____

GRANDPA'S Portrait
by ME

Portraits

MY Portrait
by GRANDPA

My favorite holiday is:
- ☐ Thanksgiving
- ☐ Independence Day
- ☐ Halloween
- ☐ Groundhog Day
- ☐ _____

How does your family celebrate this holiday?

_____

_____

On my birthday, I always:
- ☐ open presents
- ☐ eat cake and ice cream
- ☐ blow out candles
- ☐ make a wish
- ☐ _____

Draw or write about the best holiday or birthday you can remember.

Traditions!

What is Grandpa's favorite holiday and why?

_____

_____

How did his family celebrate this holiday when he was little?

_____

_____

What traditions did Grandpa pass on to his own family?

_____

_____

When Grandpa was little, how did he celebrate his birthday?

_____

_____

Draw or write about the best holiday or birthday you can remember.

Our Family Tree

My great-grandmother

My great-grandfather

My grandmother

My mother

My father

My brothers and sisters

Me

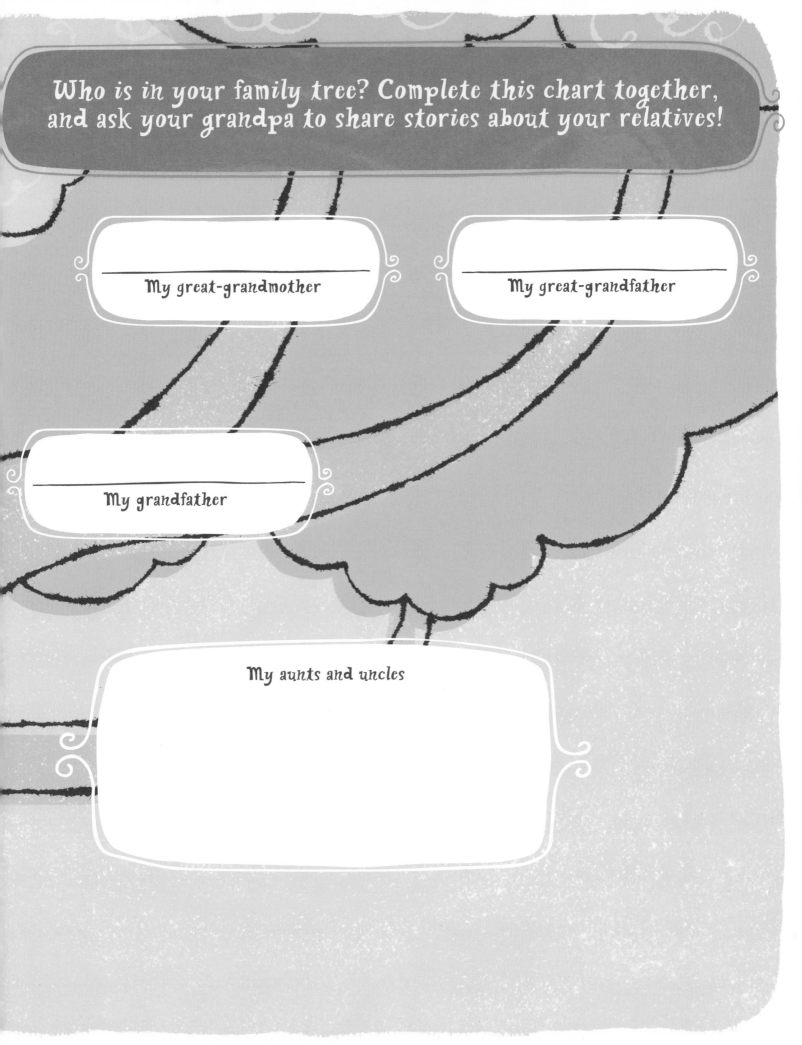

Who is in your family tree? Complete this chart together, and ask your grandpa to share stories about your relatives!

My great-grandmother

My great-grandfather

My grandfather

My aunts and uncles

Snuggle up with Grandpa and ask him to tell you about his family's history. You're sure to find out lots of things you never knew!

Where did your ancestors come from?

_____

Where was Grandpa born?

_____

Where did Grandpa grow up?

_____

What kind of jobs did your grandpa's parents have?

_____

What about your grandpa's grandparents? What did they do?

_____

Here are some things Grandpa learned from his parents:

_____

_____

Here are some things Grandpa wants me to know:

_____

_____

History

Ask Grandpa to tell you a story he remembers from childhood. It may be a story his parents or grandparents told him. It might be one that was read to him. It could even be a song or a joke. Draw a picture to illustrate Grandpa's story.

How is daily life different now than it was when Grandpa was a boy?
Write how many there are of the following things:

In my house we have a lot of stuff!

_____ bathrooms

_____ TVs

_____ phones

_____ computers

In Grandpa's childhood home, he had:

_____ bathrooms

_____ TVs

_____ phones

_____ computers

How I get to school: _____

How Grandpa got to school: _____

Things Were

My favorite games to play are:

_____

_____

When Grandpa was a little boy, his favorite games to play were:

_____

_____

The first movie I ever saw in the theater was _____

I was _____ years old.

The first movie Grandpa saw in the theater was _____

He was _____ years old.

My favorite book is _____

When Grandpa was little, his favorite book was _____

For breakfast, I usually eat _____

When Grandpa was a kid, he ate _____

My allowance is _____

When he was little, Grandpa's allowance was _____

Home Sweet

When I grow up, I want to live:

- ☐ in a house
- ☐ in an apartment
- ☐ on a boat
- ☐ in a tent
- ☐ _____

It will be:

- ☐ in a big city
- ☐ in a small town
- ☐ way out in the country
- ☐ in outer space
- ☐ _____

My home will look like this:

Home

When Grandpa was little, he lived:

- ☐ in a house
- ☐ in an apartment
- ☐ in a cabin
- ☐ in a tent
- ☐ _____

Grandpa's home was:

- ☐ in a big city
- ☐ in a small town
- ☐ way out in the country
- ☐ in outer space
- ☐ _____

It looked like this:

Do you have a secret hideout or a favorite place? Maybe it's your room or a special place outside. Did Grandpa have one as a boy? Describe these places, then imagine what the perfect secret hideout for the two of you would look like.

Here's what my favorite place is like:

_____

_____

Here's what Grandpa's favorite place was like when he was little:

_____

_____

Our secret hideout would be a:

- ☐ tree house
- ☐ fort
- ☐ cave
- ☐ submarine
- ☐ castle tower
- ☐ _____

If it could be anywhere, our secret hideout would be:

- ☐ in the jungle
- ☐ in an enchanted forest
- ☐ on top of a mountain
- ☐ deep underground
- ☐ at the bottom of the ocean
- ☐ _____

Two

Inside our secret hideout we'd have:

- ☐ bean bags and lava lamps
- ☐ tons of computers and spy equipment
- ☐ basic survival tools and a fire pit
- ☐ lots of books and toys
- ☐ royal thrones and marble statues
- ☐ _____

Who would be allowed into our hideout?

- ☐ nobody but us
- ☐ our family
- ☐ everybody
- ☐ _____

Draw a picture of your secret hideout.

No need to study for this pop quiz—it's all about fun! Answer these questions, then break out those red pens and start grading! Put a gold star next to all the right answers.

All About Grandpa!

1. Is Grandpa left-handed or right-handed?_____

2. What is Grandpa's favorite hobby?_____

3. Does he collect anything? If yes, what?_____

4. Does Grandpa have any brothers or sisters? If yes, how many?_____

5. What would he do if he had a million dollars?_____

6. What color are Grandpa's eyes?_____

7. If Grandpa could have one magical power, what would it be?

☐ ability to fly
☐ invisibility
☐ able to read others' minds
☐ super strength
☐ _____

8. Can Grandpa whistle?_____

9. What is Grandpa's favorite color? _____

10. What kind of car does Grandpa drive?_____

Quiz!

All About Me!

1. Am I left-handed or right-handed? _____

2. What is my favorite hobby? _____

3. Do I collect anything? If yes, what? _____

4. Can I roll my tongue? _____

5. What would I do if I had a million dollars? _____

6. What color are my eyes? _____

7. If I could have one magical power, what would it be?

   ☐ ability to fly
   ☐ invisibility
   ☐ able to read others' minds
   ☐ super strength
   ☐ _____

8. Can I whistle? _____

9. What is my favorite color? _____

10. What is my favorite subject at school? _____

Our Faves

Grandpa   Me

Favorite food: _____   _____

Favorite animal: _____   _____

Favorite thing to do for fun: _____   _____

Favorite movie: _____   _____

Favorite TV show: _____   _____

Favorite sport: _____   _____

My favorite activity to do with Grandpa:

_____

_____

Grandpa's favorite activity as a kid:

_____

_____

and Raves

My favorite story about Grandpa:

Grandpa's favorite story about me:

From the time you wake up until the time you go to sleep...just think of all the awesome things you and Grandpa could do together! Would you go to a movie and then get ice cream? Or would you do something crazy, like travel to the moon or take a submarine to the bottom of the ocean? Write it or draw it. And have fun!

_____

_____

_____

_____

_____

_____

_____

_____

_____

_____

With Grandpa

I can:

- ☐ stand on my head
- ☐ cross my eyes
- ☐ ride a bike
- ☐ give excellent hugs
- ☐ jump really high

- ☐ sing the entire national anthem
- ☐ win a staring contest
- ☐ play checkers
- ☐ name all the state capitals
- ☐ make people laugh

Three things I am really good at:

1. _____

2. _____

3. _____

My secret talent:

_____

Three things I want to learn to do:

1. _____

2. _____

3. _____

Talented

Grandpa can:

- [ ] sing the entire national anthem
- [ ] build a fire
- [ ] use a chainsaw
- [ ] fix things around the house
- [ ] give excellent hugs
- [ ] fall asleep sitting up
- [ ] speak a foreign language
- [ ] tell a good joke
- [ ] name the last ten presidents
- [ ] make people laugh

Three things Grandpa is really good at:

1. _____

2. _____

3. _____

Grandpa's secret talent:

_____

Three things Grandpa wants to teach me:

1. _____

2. _____

3. _____

Places I've lived:

_____

_____

_____

Places Grandpa has lived:

_____

_____

_____

Places I'd like to visit:

_____

_____

_____

Places Grandpa would like to visit:

_____

_____

_____

Draw your favorite place to be together.

Done That

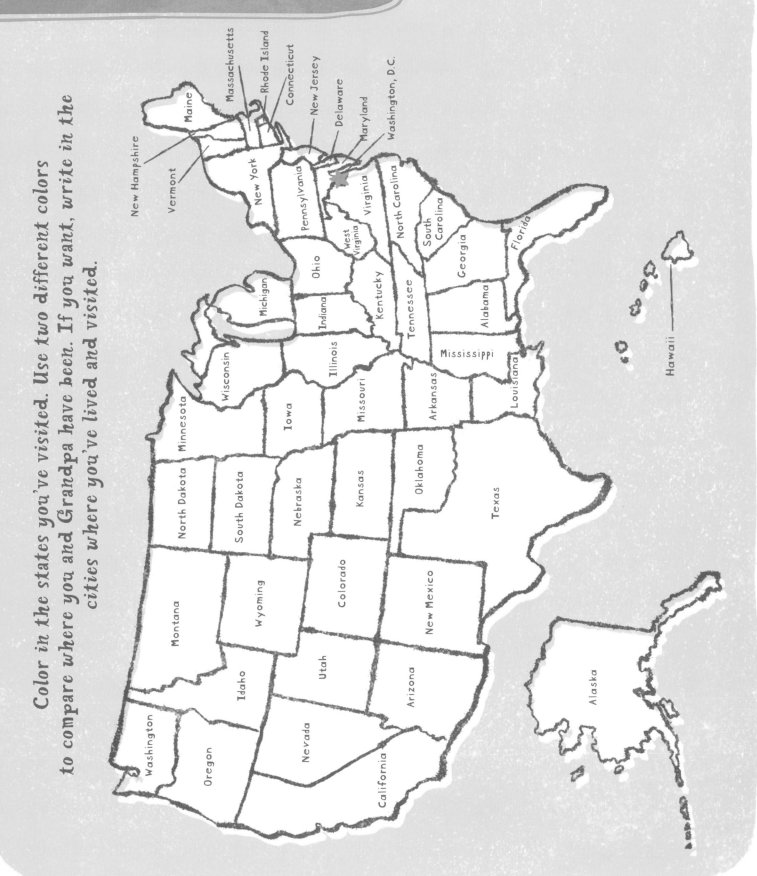

Color in the states you've visited. Use two different colors to compare where you and Grandpa have been. If you want, write in the cities where you've lived and visited.

The best advice my grandpa ever gave me was:

_____

_____

I taught Grandpa how to:

- ☐ check his e-mail
- ☐ play video games
- ☐ wiggle his nose
- ☐ make macaroni and cheese
- ☐ _____
- ☐ _____

I can always make Grandpa laugh when I:

_____

_____

Grandpa makes me laugh when he:

_____

_____

One thing my grandpa always says is:

_____

_____

My grandpa taught me to:

- ☐ swim
- ☐ build a birdhouse
- ☐ wiggle my ears
- ☐ play chess
- ☐ _____
- ☐ _____

Grandpa believes the best way to be happy is:

_____

_____

According to Grandpa, the three most important things in life are:

1. _____
2. _____
3. _____

Grandpa thinks you should never leave home without:

_____

What if you were going on a long vacation and could only take three things with you. What three items would you bring?

1. _____

2. _____

3. _____

What if you were president of the United States and Grandpa was your V.P.? What would be your first order of business?

_____

_____

What if you could only eat one thing for the rest of your life? What would you eat?

_____

_____

What if you were a celebrity? How would your life be different?

_____

_____

What if you could only eat three things for the rest of your life? What would you eat?

1. _____

2. _____

3. _____

What if you could travel through time? Where would you go?

_____

_____

What if you could draw things and make them come to life? What would you draw?

On these pages, attach your favorite photos of you and your grandpa.
Then write some funny captions together.

Me & Grandpa

Me & Grandpa

If you and your grandpa had fun
filling out this book,
Hallmark would love to hear from you.

Please send your comments to:
Hallmark Book Feedback
P.O. Box 419034
Mail Drop 215
Kansas City, MO 64141

Or e-mail us at:
booknotes@hallmark.com